WHY DIDN'T IT WORK?

Help for Christians Who are Struggling with Their Faith

WHY DIDN'T IT WORK?

Help for Christians Who are Struggling with Their Faith

Tiffany McCormick

I dedicate this book to my husband and my children; may the Word always work in your lives spiritually, relationally, and financially!

Table of Contents

Acknowledgments

I would like to acknowledge my husband for supporting me and my mom for being an honest cheerleader throughout this process. I would also like to acknowledge my friends and my pastor for believing in the work of the Holy Spirit through this book.

01

CHAPTER

Love Never Fails

In the past, I often wondered why things didn't work for me the way they seemed to work for others or the way it says it should in the Bible. Why didn't it work when I stood on the Word and believed for a spouse, or healing, or for some money to come in, but time went by, and I didn't feel as if I saw any fruit, but it seemed as if everyone else was getting married, healed, and prospering. Why didn't it work when I had faith and applied for several jobs but didn't get one, and my bills were overdue? Why didn't it work when the Word says ask and you shall receive? I felt like I was asking, and asking, and asking, but I didn't get any direction. I would sometimes stay up all night crying and praying, but I wasn't any closer to an answer than I was before. Why didn't it work? And more importantly, why didn't it work for ME?

I was extremely frustrated, and my faith started to take a hit. I wasn't spending time with God the way I should, and I started questioning what I believed. God used my pastor and other leaders in my church, Brother Moore, and the free word supply at Faith Life Church, books, friends, family, songs, and life situations to lead me on this journey of learning why it didn't work and how to get consistent results.

I had to be completely persuaded that God is real and what the Bible says is true. That may seem too basic for some, but when things are not working as you expect them to, questions will come to your mind whether you think them yourself or Satan puts them there. When you feel like you have sacrificed and obeyed God, but you struggle to have enough money to keep the lights on, and you read Mark 10:28-30 (NLT), which says, "Then Peter began to speak up. "We've given up everything to follow you," he said. "Yes," Jesus replied, "and I assure you that everyone who has given up house or brothers or sisters or mother or father or children or property, for my sake and for the Good News, will receive now in return a hundred times as many houses, brothers, sisters, mothers, children, and property—along with persecution. And in the world to come that person will have eternal life." Yet instead of a hundredfold, you get evicted, your car repossessed, your paychecks garnished, or whatever else happens, so it's hard not to wonder if it actually works. Especially if you have friends or family members who aren't doing the right thing, or you see people who you know to be sinners and unbelievers on social media seemingly enjoying life. That's just adding insult to injury!

Then, you have some Christians say I know both how to be abased, and I know how to abound, or it is easier for a camel to go through the eye of a needle than for a rich man to enter into the kingdom of God and act like they're satisfied with what they have, but you know some of them are pretending because you can see it on their face, in their body language, and how they act when they get more money or stuff. To be even more honest, it really angers me when I see racists, who claim to be Christian, getting privileged treatment and great jobs with high salaries, support from the community, and big houses, but people that look like me are being killed in the streets, our children are hurting, and we are treated as if we're not human. Not to mention the microaggressions we face every day, often from those same Christians. But I'm supposed to believe that God is just, and the just shall live by faith.

Or what if you're believing for a spouse and it's hard to even find a decent date that won't cheat on you and will be a valuable addition to you spiritually, relationally, and financially, not a burden. Or if you're trying to hold yourself, dress modestly, and treat people right, but it looks like the ones who are sleeping around, dressing provocatively, and mistreating people are always in a relationship, or they're getting married. Not to mention, so many marriages are ending in divorce, and people are saying they fell out of love or giving advice that "love isn't enough, you need more than that." But you're supposed to believe that "love never fails." Those are just examples, but you get my point. I had to cry out to God and ask why it didn't work for me!

After thinking more deeply about it, I realized that what my heart was really wrestling with was whether God loved me like a father or not. Yes, I believed Him to be my creator and savior who sent Jesus to die for my sins, but did He love me like the father mentioned in Luke 11:13 (KJV) that says, "If ye then, being evil, know how to give good gifts unto your children: how much more shall your heavenly Father give Holy Spirit to them that ask him." Again, I had to be completely persuaded that God is real and what the Bible says is true, every single book, every single chapter, every single verse. God is GOOD! So, no matter what happens (or doesn't happen), He is right, and I'm on His side. God started me on a journey that I'm still on to understand what was happening and why the Word wasn't consistently working in my life.

The first step in my personal journey began with me being sick in college. During the first semester of my freshman year, I got sick with something different almost every week for almost two months. I finally went to the on-campus doctor, and among the other issues, she mentioned that I probably had dysmenorrhea, which could be a sign of endometriosis. I didn't know what any of that meant, so I looked it up on WebMD and what I read had me so scared that I just chose to ignore it and not talk about it at the time, but my health issues became a weight pressing down on me. During all of that, my boyfriend from high school (he went to a different college) broke up with me. I had always been a straight-A student, but I was failing my classes, and socially, I didn't feel like I fit in anywhere; I was mentally in a really bad space. Moderate depression is what I was really going through because my school and social activities were significantly impacted, but I was too young to realize it at the time, and no one at Tech knew me well enough, and my friends and family were too far away to notice that I had changed.

I was on the BSO (Black Student Organizations) email list at the time, and I saw an email advertising about a Bible study that G.I.F.T.E.D. (God's Influence Flowing Through Every Disciple) was hosting, and I figured I might as well go because I wasn't getting any results from studying all night. Plus, I grew up in a Christian household, and though we didn't go to church much, and I couldn't recall ever going to a Bible study before, I was interested to see what it was like. I don't remember exactly what was said, but many times throughout the sermon, I felt like the pastor was talking directly to me. In the end, he said, "If you feel like I was talking directly to you, that's because God is talking to you through me as a vessel and He wants you to join His kingdom; come down and accept salvation and we will pray for you and with you."

My heart started burning, I immediately started crying, and I knew that the pastor was talking to me. I went down to accept salvation, and I felt peace like I had never felt before in my entire life! After that, it didn't matter what was going on, who I needed to cancel on, what needed to be rescheduled — I was going to Bible study. I didn't know the scripture at the time, but it was like the man who found the pearl of great price that sold everything he had to buy it. The pastor, who eventually became my spiritual father, began teaching a series on prayer basics and how to pray effectively, and I was soaking it up like a dry, thirsty sponge. These lessons became seeds that God used to start me on a journey to growing as a Christian and seeing things work in my life.

02

CHAPTER

My Heart

I eventually joined G.I.F.T.E.D., and a few years later when I was in my senior year, I found my old notes, and I was practicing the prayer basics I was taught and while I was in prayer, I thought about an incident that happened earlier that day with a cute black guy from one of my math classes and the thought came to me that I should probably apologize. I didn't realize it at the time, but that was Holy Spirit speaking to me and showing me what to do. When I saw him again, we were in a small group talking about studying for our class. I used that situation as a way to apologize for what I said the prior day, and we eventually became friends. Shortly thereafter, he suggested that I listen to the sermon series "Spirit Led" by Brother Moore from Faith Life Church and let him know what I thought about it. Honestly, I wasn't really interested in listening to it. Still, I thought he was cute, and he was a Christian who actually knew scripture, so I figured I would listen to give me an excuse to reach out and talk to him more.

My motives were completely wrong, and I can only laugh at myself as I look back on it but thank God I listened because the series talked about things that can get in the way of being led by the Holy Spirit and what He revealed to me was that my heart was holding me back. For me, there are times when it's not clear what God wants me to do, and it's not always as easy as asking God then immediately hearing the Word and running with it. Heart issues tend to get in the way and make it harder than it should be to hear from God. So often, I have to prepare my heart to receive. When my heart is not ready, just like in our natural bodies where plaque can build up and keep the blood from flowing and eventually cause a heart attack, there are issues within my heart that keep me from having a clear and flowing heart channel to the Lord. Here are a few common heart problems that God showed me I needed to fix:

Hardened Heart

"They are darkened in their understanding and separated from the life of God because of the ignorance that is in them due to the hardening of their hearts" Ephesians 4:1 (NIV).

When our hearts are hardened, our understanding is darkened, meaning the Word that's supposed to light our path cannot work because we are in the dark. What is a "hardened heart," and how do we know if our heart is hard? Your heart may be hardened when your life feels like this "'Listen carefully but do not understand. Watch closely but learn nothing.' Harden the hearts of these people. Plug their ears and shut their eyes. That way, they will not see with their eyes, nor hear with their ears, nor understand with their hearts." Isaiah 6:9-10 (NLT)

Whenever things aren't connecting, or they don't make sense, we should check to see the state of our hearts. Hebrews 3:7-9 (NLT) says "That is why the Holy Spirit says, 'Today when you hear his voice, don't harden your hearts as Israel did when they rebelled when they tested me in the wilderness. There your ancestors tested and tried my patience, even though they saw my miracles for forty years'". Even centuries after that generation of Israelites died in the wilderness, we are still being warned against hardening our hearts lest we be hardened through the deceitfulness of sin and can't hear the voice of God.

When I was in church, I noticed a married couple having problems. After service, I talked with my mom, and she said she was going to pray for that couple because she noticed something seemed off with them. I said, "Oh, okay, yeah, I noticed, too." She asked me if I was going to pray for them, and I said, "No, I don't feel led to do that." Then she said, "Well, just check and see."

So, I closed my eyes to pray, and I had nothing. No compassion, not a single scripture, not a thought, not even the standard "God help them." I was just looking at the back of my eyelids. My heart was hardened towards them because I felt like they deserved to be miserable. After all, their decisions led them to where they were. But the Word says to owe no man anything but to love one another, and I was not acting in love towards them. I needed to go to God and ask Him to soften my heart towards them because I didn't feel anything emotionally, so I thought I wasn't being led, but really, God is the potter, and we are the clay, and I was hard clay in that area so God could not shape me or use me in the way that He wanted to.

Prayer for a softened heart

Input whatever situation or name that pertains to you in the blank and believe by faith that God will help soften your heart. *Father, thank you for revealing the truth of my heart to me. I repent for my hard heart, and I ask that you soften my heart towards _____. I stand on Your Word in Ezekiel 1:19-20. You said that You would put a new spirit within me and take away my stony, stubborn heart and give me a tender and responsive heart so that I can walk in your statutes, keep your ordinances, and do them. I believe by faith that I receive your forgiveness and the grace to do what You say even when it gets hard. Thank you, Holy Spirit, for leading me, convicting me, and comforting me. In the name of Jesus, Amen.*

Unclean Heart

We can also have an unclean heart. Psalms 51:10 (NLT) says, "Create in me a clean heart, O God, and renew a right spirit within me." David is asking God to create a clean heart in him, which implies that his heart is not clean, and so it can be with us. When our heart is hardened, oftentimes we really don't feel much, if anything at all, but when it's not clean, it's an active feeling.

In Matthew 15:10-11 (NLT), Jesus is speaking to the crowd of scribes and Pharisees, and He says, "Hear and understand: Not what goes into the mouth defiles a man; but what comes out of the mouth, this defiles a man." Here the use of defile comes from the Greek word koinoó, which means to make common and is used as making unclean, pollute, desecrate, or treat as unclean. An unclean heart is seen by the words that come out of your mouth because out of the abundance of the heart, the mouth speaks! Even if you haven't verbally said the words, but you have the thoughts, it's the same. An unclean heart taints the Word we receive, and it poisons our thoughts and our words, so we must remember that death and life lie in the power of the tongue, and we do not want our tongue to speak death.

During my freshman year of college, a couple of months after I started my walk with Christ, I stopped being friends with a person I had been friends with for years and had known since middle school over a guy she was dating that I introduced her to. She thought I was trying to get with her boyfriend at the time behind her back. I felt as if she should have known I wasn't trying to date him because she should have known me well enough to know that I wouldn't try to date my friends' boyfriend, much less while I'm trying to date his close friend! In addition, I had no idea she was even feeling that way because instead of talking to me about it, she spoke with another person, and that person made a very negative post on social media about me being a fake friend. That was my first time hearing that she had issues with me, and I was angry and hurt by that because I felt like she had been talking maliciously about me behind my back. So basically, our friendship ended there.

Anytime I saw them, or if they came up in conversation, I would say something sarcastic or mean. Though I eventually stopped saying negative things, I definitely kept thinking negative thoughts. It was almost as if she could not be happy anymore for the rest of her life because I felt like she slighted me. My heart was UNCLEAN! It kept me from hearing God clearly and doing what I was supposed to do. I didn't deal with it for years, and I thought I had gotten over it until I found out that they broke up, and I laughed to myself when I found out, and Holy Spirit said, "Do not rejoice over their heartbreak. Their hearts are hurting; pray for them." Shortly thereafter, I found this scripture in Proverbs 24:17 (NLT) that says, "Don't rejoice when your enemies fall; don't be happy when they stumble" and knew that it was God and that I needed to forgive her and move on.

Prayer for a clean heart

Input whatever situation or name that pertains to you in the blank and believe by faith that God will help cleanse your heart. *God, I repent for having an unclean heart and speaking and thinking negative and wicked things about _____. Holy Spirit, I ask that you create in me a clean heart and renew a right spirit within me towards _____ and that you set a watch at my mouth so that I am holy in all manner of conversation as the Word says in 1 Peter 1:15. The enemy shall no longer use me to speak against your people, and my heart will be pure and holy towards them. I thank you for new mercies every day, and I ask that you keep me when it gets hard so that I can be steadfast, unmovable, and always abounding in You. In Jesus' name, Amen.*

Unwilling/Rebellious Heart

In the old testament, we read about the children of Israel being delivered from the Egyptians and going to possess the promised land. God told them in Exodus 3:8 (KJV) that, "I am come down to deliver them out of the hand of the Egyptians, and to bring them up out of that land unto a good and large land, unto a land flowing with milk and honey; unto the place of the Canaanites, and the Hittites, and the Amorites, and the Perizzites, and the Hivites, and the Jebusites." Yet, in Numbers 13, when the twelve spies were sent out, and ten of them came back with an evil report about the land and the giants that were there, the Israelites cried and wept all night and murmured against Moses and Aaron. As a result, God said that except for Caleb and Joshua, none of them would see the promised land, but they would wander in the wilderness. Just like it states in Deuteronomy 1:26 (NIV), "But you were unwilling to go up; you rebelled against the command of the LORD your God." When our hearts are unwilling to serve or do what God tells us or asks us to do, we are in rebellion, and a rebellious heart disqualifies us from the promises of God. This stopped the Israelites from obtaining the promises, and it can also stop us.

Once I had a conflict with a female member of my church because of my friendship with her boyfriend, and our pastor suggested we meet to figure out a way to work everything out so that she could feel comfortable with his and my friendship. At first, I was just annoyed. I was thinking, *why can't we all just be adults? I have my own set of people I'm dating* (one of whom eventually became my husband). *I'm not trying to take him from you. You're doing too much, but whatever.* Eventually, I agreed. But as the day wore on and I thought more about it, I became extremely unwilling.

Why did I need to make sure she was comfortable and clear the air with her over a problem she created? I felt like I was the victim because he and I mostly just talked about the Word and sermons we listened to. He even told me about him planning to marry her, and I mentioned getting them tickets to a nice place for their honeymoon because I worked for Delta Air Lines at the time, so it could be my gift for them to enjoy. Yet, she and her people were talking about me and spreading lies about me, so why did I need to be the one to extend the olive branch and help her out. She clearly had a strong support system and was going to do what she wanted to do regardless of what I said or did, so no, I wasn't going to go. I was not going to help her or help them or clear any sort of confusion. That was their issue now, not mine. As far as I was concerned, they made their bed.

I eventually got so worked up that my whole body was tense, my face was hot, my chest was tight, and the more I thought about it, it felt like the frustration and anger were rising in me from the sole of my feet! Then the Lord said, "Do it for me," and immediately the tears started rolling down my face, and the fight was just taken out of me because He was so gentle, and it felt like love literally wrapped around me. He revealed to me that the main reason I was unwilling was that I was envious that she was about to get married, but, in my opinion, I was a "better" Christian than her, so it should be my turn first. God reminded me that I need to walk by faith and not by sight. So, I agreed to meet with her, and I was glad I listened to God because it helped me see more clearly what was going on and start forgiving them.

I didn't start forgiving the rest of the group, though. That took a lot more time because I wasn't obedient when God asked me to make peace with them.

Prayer for an obedient heart

Input whatever situation or name pertains to you in the blank and believe by faith that God will help your heart become more willing. *Abba Father! Because I am yours, you sent forth the Spirit of Jesus into my heart. Psalms 51:17 (KJV) says a broken and a contrite heart, O God, thou wilt not despise, so I humble myself right now and repent for my rebellion and disobedience regarding_____. I am standing on Your Word in Romans 6:17-18 (KJV) that says, "But God be thanked, that I was a servant of sin, BUT I have obeyed from the heart the teaching I was given and being made free from sin, I am the servant of righteousness." Now I come boldly to the throne of grace, that I may obtain mercy and find grace to help me in my time of need. Thank you for loving me. In Jesus' name, Amen.*

A heart to receive

If we want to hear God clearly and have the faith to stand on what He says, our heart posture must be aligned with His Word. I had to ask God to help soften, cleanse, and purify my heart towards the people in those situations (and many others) because I was not operating in love. Holy Spirit constantly reveals my heart to me, so I have started to recognize signs that something is going on with my heart, and I've learned a few things to do to keep my heart in check.

The first thing I have to do is physically change my posture. I need to align my body so that I am in a submitted position, whether that's bowing my head, kneeling down on the floor, raising my arms as if in worship, or whatever. There's something about being in a physical position of submission and worship that also helps me submit my heart. When my body is tense and unyielding, it is easy for the enemy to keep speaking to me, and it's harder for me to fix my heart.

Another thing I have to do is fast. It can be skipping a meal, turning off the TV, stepping away from social media, or whatever I need to do to crucify my flesh. While I'm fasting, I also turn on some music and sing and dance to praise and worship God and combine it with prayer during certain prayer watches. This tends to clear my mind and reset my thoughts to allow me to focus.

Last but certainly not least, I look up some scriptures related to what I'm feeling and read those slowly and intentionally to focus on the voice of God and drown out any distractions. My goal is to meditate on the Word and to hide those scriptures in my heart that I may not sin against God.

I pray that this chapter urges you to evaluate the condition of your heart and ask Holy Spirit to reveal what is in your heart so that you can begin to hear what God wants to tell you and have faith that what He says for you to do will work.

03

CHAPTER

My Faith

After I began the lifelong process of working on my heart, God used that same friend from math class to ask me to listen to "How to Receive Anything" by Brother Moore. After the success of the last recommendation, I had better motives. I wanted to listen to it for my own knowledge and understanding this time. One of the points in the series talks about using your faith to reach out and receive whatever it is you're believing for, and at the same time, my pastor was going over studying the Word and believing God in every area of our lives. God used those situations to reveal to me that I needed to work on my faith. If I wanted the Word to work in my life, I needed to believe that it would; something that is much easier said than done.

Then I got stuck because I thought I was hearing the Word. I was going to church and taking notes, praying, reading my Bible, and even fasting every so often, so what was I missing? I went to Romans 10:17 (KJV) which says, "So then faith cometh by hearing, and hearing by the word of God" I looked it up, and 'faith' in that verse is trust, confidence, belief, and full persuasion, and 'the Word' in that verse refers to the anointed Rhema word. So stated differently, confidence comes by hearing the anointed spoken utterance. If I needed more faith, I had to hear the Word of Christ, the anointed one. I started thinking about that scripture and going over what I had been hearing, and then it hit me. I was trying to believe for things without knowing what God said about them specifically. I was reading the *logos* or the written Word but not getting the Rhema or the spoken word/utterance specifically for me and my particular situation. So, after all those years, why didn't it work? I didn't know His Word for my situation, so I couldn't have faith in what He said.

Unbelief

I began talking to God about areas where I was in doubt, but I was actually trying to justify why I didn't believe and how it was natural or human to have some level or a small amount of doubt or skepticism because we can't just believe any and everything, we need confirmation and unction from Holy Spirit. I was trying to tell the Lord that He did not understand being a human and how we have doubts sometimes. I can only shake my head at the nerve I had. Being the holy, gentle, pure, and loving Father He is, God said to me very plainly, "There is no excuse for unbelief." Then He reminded me of something Brother Moore taught in a sermon, that there are at least two types of unbelief: ignorant and evil, "Ignorance needs instruction, rebellion needs correction."

When Paul was writing to Timothy in 1 Timothy 1:13 (YLT) he said, "I, who before was speaking evil, and persecuting, and insulting, but I found kindness, because being ignorant, I did it in unbelief." Now compare that to Hebrews 3:12 (KJV) which states, "Take heed, brethren, lest there be in any of you an evil heart of unbelief, in departing from the living God." Then Paul says that God swore they would not enter into His rest because of unbelief. The difference between Paul and the children of Israel is that Paul obtained mercy due to his ignorance and got instruction, and the Israelites did not because they knew what was right in their hearts but chose not to have faith which was evil and needed correction.

Here are five signs that we're walking in unbelief or have stopped having faith. This is not an exhaustive list, but just some slightly more uncommon ones that God illuminated to me:

1. **We don't have joy and peace**- Romans 15:13 (KJV) says, "Now the God of hope fill you with all joy and peace in believing, that ye may abound in hope, through the power of the Holy Ghost." Isaiah 55:12 (KJV) says, "You will go out in joy and be led forth in peace; the mountains and hills will burst into song before you, and all the trees of the field will clap their hands." For me, I like to think of it as going somewhere in a car. The amount of peace I have about something is like the odometer, it tracks the miles I've gone, and the more peace I have, the further I can go. Joy is like the speedometer. The more joy I have, the faster

I feel like I'm going. We should keep track of how much joy and peace we have because it's an indicator of whether we're operating in faith or if we need to stop and fill up.

2. **We are hiding what's really going on-** When we don't want others to know that we're struggling or even that the situation has gotten worse due to fear or pride or whatever our issue is, we should check whether we're operating in faith or not. This is different from releasing things prematurely or to the wrong people; it's driven by impure motives. When we tell people what God told us He would do for us, then it's out there, so if it does not happen, we can feel embarrassed, ashamed, or foolish, and we can be ridiculed, mocked, and deemed untrustworthy. How many times have we heard someone say, "I'm believing God to heal my loved one" or, "God said He's going to heal them"? Then next thing we know, that loved one dies. It's such a heartbreaking faith killer. I used to cringe and flinch a little when I heard those types of declarations, not knowing if what they said would happen or not. So, then we decide that if we don't say anything, no one will know if it doesn't work, but if I'm 100% certain that something will happen with no wavering, no doublemindedness, no shadow of turning, AND God tells me to speak it, then I will shout it from the rooftops!

3. **We don't act like it will happen**- Faith without works is dead. Not that we can earn our salvation through works, but our actions are the fruit of our faith. I'm going to go swimming, then I'll bring a swimsuit, and that's how we are when we believe something is going to happen, we prepare as if it will. When we do not prepare for it to come, that's an indicator that we might not believe that it's going to happen. Or we're not sure God is going to do it the way He said He would, so we try to do our own thing just in case, and we set up a plan B. There is no plan B when you believe what God said is plan A.

4. **We are worrying**- Worrying is evidence of little faith, and it can be summed up in Matthew 6:27-30 (NLT) which says, "Can all your worries add a single moment to your life? And why worry about your clothing? Look at the lilies of the field and how they grow. They don't work or make their clothing, yet Solomon was not dressed as beautifully as they are in all his glory. And if God cares so wonderfully for wildflowers that are here today and thrown into the fire tomorrow, he will certainly care for you. Why do you have so little faith?"

5. **We are speaking against it**- Another indicator that we may be in unbelief or have stopped believing is in the

words we say. It's from the abundance of the heart that the mouth speaks. If I believe that God is going to meet all my needs AND I'll have money left over to buy the top of the line or premium version of something I want, I wouldn't go around talking about how I'm broke or can't afford to pay my bills because, in my heart, I'm not broke, my every need is met, every want is fulfilled, and every desire satisfied even if I don't see it in the natural yet; I continue to speak life over my situation expecting it to happen.

Seeing is believing

Faith is spoken of so often in Christian circles that I misunderstood some key aspects of faith and I hope to clarify some things for you as well. How many times have we scoffed at something and said, "I'll believe it when I see it" or "seeing is believing"? I did not realize that was completely against what real faith is, and saying that only showed that I didn't have any faith. Hebrews 11:1 (KJV) states, "Now faith is the substance of things hoped for, the evidence of things not seen." I had been trying to SEE it to dictate if I believed it and if God said it. It was so subtle that I didn't realize I was doing it. I let that sink into my heart so I would start to look for a tangible or physical manifestation of what He said before I would truly believe, but that is not what the Word says. Faith is the evidence of things NOT seen.

When I was working at my first job out of college, I eventually started to hate the job I had. I enjoyed the company, my co-workers and boss were nice, and I didn't have any workplace drama, but I loathed going to work every day and doing what I did. So, I began praying for a new job. Month after month passed, and I was still there but continually applying for jobs and I was getting interviews but no offers.

More months passed, and I started getting frustrated. I turned towards options to go back to school, thinking that maybe I couldn't find a job because God was telling me to go to graduate school. Still, I could not get a clear direction on which school to go to and what degree to get, so I started studying for the GMAT (Graduate Management Admission Test). However, I was not really motivated, so I was still applying for jobs every so often or trying to start my own business. I was being led by what I could see happening (or not happening). If I didn't get an interview or a new job, then that's not what I'm supposed to do. If I get accepted into school, then that's what God wants me to do. So, once I realized that I was trying to SEE something instead of believing, I opened my heart and asked the Holy Spirit what I should be doing? Then the answer hit me like a flash of lighting. Holy Spirit said I was looking for what to do at step 3, but I skipped step 1. He said that step 1 was to quit my current job. The first thing that next morning, I put in my notice and had a conversation with my boss once he made it to the office, then by 4 p.m. that afternoon, I got a call to interview for a role, and Holy Spirit said this is the one. Within two weeks, I got the new role, and my salary was practically DOUBLE what I was making before, and it had better benefits.

How to get faith

"But they have not all obeyed the gospel. For Isaias saith, Lord, who hath believed our report? So then faith cometh by hearing, and hearing by the word of God" Romans 10:16-17 (KJV). "But they were not all obedient to the good tidings, for Isaiah saith, 'Lord, who did give credence to our report?' So then the faith is by a report, and the report through a saying of God" Romans 10:16-17 (YLT)

Another area I realized I had a faith misunderstanding in was how to get faith. I thought I was hearing the Word. Again, I was going to church, praying, reading my Bible, and trying to work on my heart, so what was I missing this time? What report was Isaiah talking about that the people didn't believe? Well, this scripture is based on Isaiah 53:1 (KJV) that says, "Who hath believed our report? and to whom is the arm of the Lord revealed?" This reminded me of the Israelites when the spies (except Caleb and Joshua) brought back an evil report about the promised land. To those who believe, the arm of the Lord is revealed to them. This is what I was missing! I didn't feel like I was operating that much different from other people in the world. Sure, I had peace and joy sometimes, and I didn't do the things I used to, but where was the life more abundantly part of having God move in my life. I thought I was operating in faith because I believed in God. Holy Spirit revealed to me that we can have faith in some areas but none in others. For example, I believed I was saved but I didn't truly believe that God would heal me. I had faith in my salvation but not my healing so the arm of the Lord was not revealed because I didn't believe the report or the Word of God in that area.

Little faith

Faith is used 245 times in the King James Version of the new testament. One story that I have seen and heard many times regarding faith was what Jesus told the disciples after they couldn't drive the demon out of the boy.

Matthew 17:19-20 (NKJV) says, "Then the disciples came to Jesus privately and said, 'Why could we not cast it out?' So Jesus said to them, 'Because of your unbelief; for assuredly, I say to you, if you have faith as a mustard seed, you will say to this mountain,

'Move from here to there,' and it will move, and nothing will be impossible for you.'"

Some translations say it's because of your little faith instead of unbelief. They wanted to know why it didn't work for them, and the lack of faith was an issue; they only needed faith the size of a mustard seed. So, when God tells us to start a business but we don't want to leave our job, we try to make it a side hustle and just do a little instead of putting our all into it because we only have a little faith. Or we go and start doing other works because we want to have something just in case God doesn't come through for us.

Feigned faith

2 Timothy 1:5 (KJV) says, "When I call to remembrance the unfeigned faith that is in thee, which dwelt first in thy grandmother Lois, and thy mother Eunice; and I am persuaded that in thee also." 1 Timothy 1:5-7 (NLT) says, "The purpose of my instruction is that all believers would be filled with love that comes from a pure heart, a clear conscience, and genuine faith (unfeigned faith). But some people have missed this whole point. They have turned away from these things and spend their time in meaningless discussions. They want to be known as teachers

of the Law of Moses, but they don't know what they are talking about, even though they speak so confidently."

Feigned in these verses come from the Greek word "anupokritos" which means unhypocritical, unfeigned, and is used "not a phony ("put on"), describing sincere behavior free from hidden agendas (selfish motives). This type of faith can be seen in many Christian circles. We act the part and say the right words, but, on the inside, we don't truly believe at the level we portray. We pretend to have faith in the impossible, but we really don't, and this is a faith killer for ourselves and those watching us.

God operates in what's real and what's true. If we want the Word to work for us, we have to do the same. God would prefer that we be either hot or cold, so if we aren't confident in something, then instead of being lukewarm where we pretend to be filled with faith, meaning we're "hot" on the outside while we're actually in unbelief or "cold' on the inside, be honest with the state of our faith. If we aren't at the level to believe God, then we should cry out like the man whose son had a dumb spirit in Mark 9:23-24 (KJV) which states, "Jesus said unto him, 'If thou canst believe, all things are possible to him that believeth.' And straightway the father of the child cried out, and said with tears, 'Lord, I believe; help thou mine unbelief.'" This man did not pretend with Jesus. He asked for help with his unbelief. Imagine how God looks to those outside of the kingdom, our children, or even others inside the body of Christ. If they see you seemingly on fire and having faith, then what you say you believe in doesn't work. After a while, their belief in God could be negatively affected, and for those who don't believe, it's just more proof that God is not real.

Faith works by love

My husband and I were having problems in our marriage, and I was praying about it (again) because we had just been having problem after problem, and I was tired of crying about it. I was going on and on about how I didn't think he was helping with the kids and wasn't being a loving husband or wasn't doing this or wasn't saying that and all these issues I was having with him. I got to the point in the conversation where I was thinking about some things my husband had said and how it hurt me, and then I had the thought, "love that man." This was the Lord telling me in a still, small voice that sounded just like one of my thoughts, what to do to help my marriage. I'm sure you can imagine that I didn't immediately jump for joy when He told me that. I laughingly scoffed. "What do you mean, God? I had been loving him. I am not the problem. The problem is him not loving me." Then I started to get a little irritated. I was thinking, why did I have to do the right thing when he's in the wrong as well? But I kept what God said to myself and hid it so I could give myself an excuse in the future when I didn't feel like doing it.

Every few weeks, "Love that man" would keep coming up, so eventually, I looked for sermons and started listening to "Keeping the Love Command," another sermon series by Brother Moore. As I listened to it and thought about what it truly means to love someone in action, I began to fear that I would be alone in the marriage, loving him but not being loved back. I started to worry that I would be doing what I was supposed to do, yet I didn't see him listening to sermons on how to love me so I felt as if he would take advantage of me and my submission. I didn't even act like I thought the marriage would get better, because I had stopped planning for our future together. BUT in the series, Brother Moore goes over John 15:10-12 (KJV) which says, "If ye keep my commandments, ye shall abide in my love; even as I have kept my Father's commandments and abide in his love. These things have I spoken unto you, that my joy might remain in you, and that your joy might be full. This is my commandment, that ye love one another, as I have loved you." This scripture was God telling me that He told me to love my husband because my joy would be full.

The enemy would try to persuade me not to do it over fear or worry that my husband will take advantage of me, run over me, or somehow abuse the fact that I'm submitting myself to him. Yet loving him as Christ loves me is a command, and I have to believe by faith that by doing it, my marriage will get better. Also, Galatians 5 says that faith works by love! So if my faith for a better marriage doesn't seem to be producing any good fruit, then one area I need to check is my love because maybe that's why my faith isn't working. If I am going to have faith and believe, then I need to operate in love. From then, I started activating my faith by taking small steps in the areas mentioned in the series, such as preferring my husbands' needs over my own based on Romans 12:10 (AMP) which states, "Be devoted to one another with [authentic] brotherly affection [as members of one family], give preference to one another in honor" and Philippians 2:3 (NLT) "Don't be selfish; don't try to impress others. Be humble, thinking of others as better than yourselves."

As I sought to incorporate more love to make my faith work, Holy Spirit would give me wisdom and tell me practical things to do, like if I'm on the way home from work, Holy Spirit will say, "shower and have marital relations with your husband tonight" or "stop by the store and buy him some soda." It's up to me to have faith and be obedient even when I'm tired or don't feel like it. I started to notice that when I was willing to do what Holy Spirit was saying and commanding my body to obey, the request wasn't as bad as I thought, or I wouldn't be as tired anymore because my obedience activated the grace to do what I was told to do. I also started planning things like our 40th birthday party (his birthday is one day before mine) and envisioning our 27th wedding anniversary (27 because we got married when we were 27, so we would have been married for half our lives) because I'm believing for it to happen. The king's heart is in the hand of the Lord, so just like God is changing my heart towards my husband, He can change my husband's heart towards me.

04

CHAPTER

My Obedience

One day I asked God what area I should be focusing on because I still hadn't been seeing consistent results, but I was trying to keep my heart clear and my faith strong. Holy Spirit led me to articles and sermons that all basically led to Deuteronomy 30:19-20a (KJV) that says, "I call heaven and earth to record this day against you, that I have set before you life and death, blessing and cursing: therefore choose life, that both thou and thy seed may live: That thou mayest love the LORD thy God, and that thou mayest obey his voice, and that thou mayest cleave unto him: for he is thy life, and the length of thy days."

We have an important role to play in what happens in our lives. We must choose life. We must choose to love and obey God. He does not force us. We have to choose His will for our lives; otherwise, we choose death. I had mistaken what it means when we say, "God is sovereign." Due to improper teaching and a worldly understanding of God, I thought it meant that God's will shall be done regardless of what I say or do, but many things involving me and my life are actually left up to my will. For example, 2 Peter 3:9 (NKJV) says, "The Lord is not slack concerning His promise, as some count slackness, but is longsuffering toward us, not willing that any should perish but that all should come to repentance." The Lord's will is that none of us perish, but people die without accepting Christ every day because there are things we have to do and a part we have to play and, in this case, that means we have to choose Jesus. We can stop the will of God from working in our lives. My pastor generally speaks on spiritual warfare a lot, and around this time, he was specifically teaching about generational curses and how disobedience in our bloodline could be keeping things from happening for us and how we must break those curses and walk in immediate obedience.

Obedience is better than sacrifice

Towards the end of Mark 3, Jesus is with the disciples and is teaching the multitude when people tell him that his mother and brothers are outside seeking Him. Jesus said that those around Him are his mother and brothers and even more to the point, whosoever shall do the will of God are His family. We should take disobedience just as seriously! When we do not do God's will, we are not His family members, and God takes disobedience seriously. In 1 Samuel 15 (KJV), God used Samuel to tell Saul to smite the Amalekites and "to utterly destroy all that they have, and spare them not; but slay both man and woman, infant and suckling, ox and sheep, camel and ass," but we read that they slew everyone but the king and "the best of the sheep, and of the oxen, and of the fatlings, and the lambs, and all that was good, and would not utterly destroy them" and because of that God told Samuel, "It repenteth me that I have set up Saul to be king:

for he is turned back from following me, and hath not performed my commandments."

Then Samuel spends a night crying and grieving. Have you ever felt when Holy Spirit was grieved? I have. This one time, I was praying and asking God what He wanted me to do for the 4th quarter of the year, and suddenly I saw an almond slice and a black pine tree-like thing spreading in it, and my heart felt like it was being torn in pieces. If you've ever gotten dumped by someone you loved, it was like that but a thousand times worse. I felt like the love of my life broke up with me, and my friends, family, and loved ones turned their back on me. I literally could not stop the tears from flowing; I could only curl up in a ball and cry. I asked God what was going on, and he told me that the evil pine tree I saw was my unbelief spreading through the almond-like black ink on a white page.

I googled "evil unbelief" and found Hebrews 3, which talks about having an evil heart of unbelief. I originally thought His issue was that I didn't have faith and Holy Spirit kept reminding me that I didn't see a mustard seed, I saw an almond slice. So, I googled "what does an almond represent in the Bible," and what stuck out to me was Numbers 17 when Aaron's rod budded with almonds to show that the Lord chose the house of Levi as a sign to the rebellious people that were murmuring against Moses and

Aaron. Then I came upon a scripture that never stood out to me before, Jeremiah 1:11-12 (KJV), which states, "Moreover the Word of the Lord came unto me, saying, 'Jeremiah, what seest thou?' And I said, 'I see a rod of an almond tree.' Then said the Lord unto me, 'Thou hast well seen for I will hasten my Word to perform it.'" He was grieved because I didn't believe in those He sent to me. A series of actions and experiences had eroded my faith in most of the leadership at my church, and it was affecting my obedience to what He told me to do there. He wanted me to reconnect to where He sent me (my church) because there was work that needed to be done quickly.

I had to lay prostrate and repent, and then I made sure I wrote down the experience so that I would never forget it. So now I'm back in 1 Samuel 15, and I'm putting myself in Samuel's shoes. I've been crying all night in grief with an aching heart, and then I go to meet Saul, and as I'm passing by, the people are excited over the spoils of war and in 1 Samuel 15:13 (KJV) it says "When Samuel finally found him, Saul greeted him cheerfully. 'May the Lord bless you,' he said. 'I have carried out the Lord's command!'" WHAT! I can just imagine how incredulous, sad, and angry Samuel probably is right now. Samuel basically said if that's the case, why do I hear the animals that are supposed to be dead? And Saul shifts the blame to the people and says, "They have brought them from the Amalekites: for the people spared the best of the sheep and of the oxen, to sacrifice unto the Lord thy God; and the rest we have utterly destroyed." Now here's the main point: 1 Samuel 15:22 (KJV) says, "And Samuel said, 'Hath the Lord as great delight in burnt offerings and sacrifices, as in obeying the voice of the Lord? **Behold, to obey is better than sacrifice, and to hearken than the fat of rams.'**"

Knowing God for myself

I thought that was the end, but then Holy Spirit spoke to me about obedience, faith, and my heart and how they work together. I can't have one or two without the other, using this example from Acts 19:13-16 (NLT) that says, "A group of Jews was traveling from town to town casting out evil spirits. They tried to use the name of the Lord Jesus in their incantation, saying, 'I command you in the name of Jesus, whom Paul preaches, to come out!'" Seven sons of Sceva, a leading priest, were doing this. But one time, when they tried it, the evil spirit replied, 'I know Jesus, and I know Paul, but who are you?' Then the man with the evil spirit leaped on them, overpowered them, and attacked them with such violence that they fled from the house, naked and battered."

Their faith and confidence were based on the God they knew through Paul instead of their own heart relationship, and their actions were disobedient because they weren't doing what God told them to do. In my heart, I needed to know who God was to me, not the God that my pastor, my spouse, my mom, Brother Moore, or whoever else preached. I couldn't just do what I had seen others do or say what they said. I needed to know what God wanted me to do and speak. That's what I could have faith in, that's the Word I needed to obey, and my God is the one I could trust with all my heart and lean not to my own understanding. Otherwise, I can't take control of the things happening in my life. I would be battered and defeated by life and the enemy every time and left wondering why the Word isn't working for me. There are several reasons for disobedience, but pride and sin are the major ones that God showed me I needed to work on:

Pride

"The Lord be high, yet hath he respect unto the lowly: but the proud he knoweth afar off." Pslams 138:6 (KJV)

Another reason it didn't work is that we are/were too prideful. We have to be careful about pride because it's really subtle, and sometimes we don't even realize we're operating in it — proud to be an American, proud of my kids, proud of my team, proud of my city, proud of myself. God hates pride. As a matter of fact, the moment when God could have used pride the way many of us do, it's when Jesus gets baptized, and God says, "this is my beloved Son, in whom I am well pleased." He does not say He's proud of Jesus, so you should watch when you use the word pride. Even with that understanding, it's not just the word itself. It's about the state of our hearts. Sometimes, it's helpful if I substitute the word *pride* for *stiff neck* when determining if I'm operating in pride or not.

"Ye stiff-necked and uncircumcised in heart and ears, ye do always resist the Holy Ghost: as your fathers did, so do ye." Acts 7:51 (KJV)

A stiff-necked person is a stubborn, obstinate person typically filled with pride. Just like the Israelites were stiff-necked after being freed from the Egyptians, we have to watch that we don't do the same. When I am prideful, I can often physically feel my back straightening, my neck stiffening up, and sometimes my nose is tilted up in the air. During those times, it helps me to physically bow my head, relax my shoulders, and refocus on God

Sin

Over the years, I've seen people get so focused on sin that they are in bondage and can't live in the freedom that grace has bought us. On the other hand, some get so caught up in grace and mercy that their attitude towards sin is too cavalier and apathetic. Yet sin is a real reason for things not working for us. I'm defining sin as missing the mark and not doing what we know to do per Strong's concordance 266. hamartia, or as James 4:17 (CEV) puts it, "If you don't do what you know is right, you have sinned." So, I believe Holy Spirit will convict you and bring up the exact sins and weights that are keeping you from moving in the things of God.

In Hebrews 12:1 (NKJV), it says, "Therefore we also since we are surrounded by so great a cloud of witnesses, let us lay aside every weight, and the sin which so easily ensnares us, and let us run with endurance the race that is set before us." Now let's imagine running a marathon, 26.2 miles. The LAST thing we need is to be running or trying to run, and we have weights on our ankles and wrists, resistance bands on our legs, heavy shoulder pads, etc., yet that's the weight and sin holding us back. We think God is trying to teach us something or work in some mysterious way, but actually, things are hard because we're in sin, or we're being crushed under the weight of generational curses.

Now add rocks randomly all over the ground, making you trip and stumble. 1 Peter 2 tells us that those rocks are the result of disobedience! So, they wouldn't even be there if we were doing what we knew to do. For me, this typically comes in some form of laziness where I don't feel like getting up and doing what I'm supposed to do, like praying during my assigned watch, reading my Bible, finishing my schoolwork, doing the laundry, etc. I just want to lay down, eat, and read manga or Korean web novels. But the Word says, "A little sleep, a little slumber, a little folding of the hands to rest—and poverty will come on you like a thief and scarcity like an armed man." We do not make it to the place where God has certain things planned for us because we're stuck in our sin, weights, or backsliding. So, we are disobedient, serving sin, and not serving God.

James 4:3 (NIV) says, "When you ask, you do not receive, because you ask with wrong motives, that you may spend what you get on your pleasures." The word pleasure comes from Strong's concordance 2237, Hédoné- a strong desire, passion. It says, "satisfaction of physical appetite has a strong negative connotation, generally referring to pleasure that is made an end in itself. That is, the satiation of bodily desires (lusts) at the expense of other things." It's not about having fun or enjoying yourself. The problem is sin, and when we do that, we sin at the expense of our relationship with God. Or we're selfish and store up stuff or hoard it for ourselves, and we don't allow God to use us to bless other people. We don't do what we know is right, at the expense of getting that healing, that deliverance, that provision, that direction, that whatever it is we're asking for.

Humility and Submission

Let's talk about submission. When Jesus was in the garden of Gethsemane, he said, "not my will but thine will be done." I had to realize that doing the will of God instead of my own is submission and to stop trying to make it more complicated than that. James 4:6-7 (ESV) says, "But he gives more grace." Therefore, it says, "God opposes the proud but gives grace to the humble. Submit yourselves therefore to God. Resist the devil, and he will flee from you." We absolutely do not want God to be our opponent; we will lose every single time without fail. Proverbs 3:34 (NKJV) says, "Surely He scorns the scornful, but gives grace to the humble." When we submit and humble ourselves to God and do His will, not our own, we will get the grace we need to resist the devil, and he will flee.

In addition to that, Jesus said in Matthew 11:28-30 (NLT), "Then Jesus said, 'Come to me, all of you who are weary and carry heavy burdens, and I will give you rest. Take my yoke upon you. Let me teach you because I am humble and gentle at heart, and you will find rest for your souls. For my yoke is easy to bear, and the burden I give you is light.'" Imagine all the attributes of Jesus that he could have used to describe himself, but He chose humility, so it speaks volumes of how important it is to be humble. From the Strong's concordance, humble is 5011 tapeinos: low-lying; it's used as humble, lowly, in position or spirit (in a good sense). We also can look at 1 Peter 3:4 (NLT), which says, "You should clothe yourselves instead with the beauty that comes from within, the unfading beauty of a gentle and quiet spirit, which is so precious to God." Many people attribute that to women, or more specifically a wife, but that gentle is the same word used as gentle that Jesus uses to describe himself as in Matthew 11.

When I was asking God why it didn't work, and those scriptures eventually came up, I realized that life (and by life, I mean being a smart, dark-skinned, black woman growing up in Georgia that didn't know how to dress, didn't know how to do her hair, and didn't know how to open her heart due to childhood trauma) had given me a hard and rough view of life, and I wasn't humble in fact, I took pride in my intelligence. I felt like I was smarter than most of my peers, and things like math were easy for me, but once I got to Georgia Tech, I felt as if everybody was smart, but I felt dumb and didn't stick out anymore. Then I had an identity crisis that lasted a couple of years because I had unknowingly built my identity around "I may be poor, ugly, and skinny, but I'm smart," but at Tech, I didn't think I was smart anymore. I was left wondering who I was. Thankfully, I started going to on-campus Bible studies, and Holy Spirit began working on my heart, and I accepted salvation. I started getting into the Word myself and forming my own relationship with God. Over time, the Lord began to show me that it's by His grace that I can do anything; it's in Him that I live, move, and have my being.

Grace

I've seen God's grace referred to as God's Riches At Christ's Expense, and it's so true. God's grace is what makes mathematical topics make sense to me. God's grace is what got me my first six-figure job. God's grace is what helps me be a wife and mom. God's grace is what gets me out of bed in the morning. God's grace is sufficient. When talking about pride and humility, we have to be careful that the enemy doesn't make us focus on ourselves. Just like a serpent, it can slide in subtly with cunning deceitfulness. That could look like us doing spiritual things like praying in tongues for hours, or tarrying for days, or fasting for weeks, and we're doing it so that we can get the power from God, and we're going to go out and do this or do that for God.

While on the surface, there doesn't seem to be anything wrong with that, we must remember that we don't do things by God, He does things by us. That's an important yet subtle distinction because we can make it about us that WE'RE going to pray, fast, and get the power to do this or that. Acts 19:11 (KJV) states, "And God wrought special miracles by the hands of Paul." God gave the power to Paul. It's Paul who was used by God. God does things by people that will yield and submit to Him, and pride will have us not seeing ourselves as we truly are.

Humility lives in the reality that apart from God, we are nothing (John 15:4), we can do nothing (John 15:5), and there's no reason for anything to exist because everything was made for Christ (John 1:3, Colossians 1:16). We can do all things THROUGH CHRIST, and all things are possible WITH GOD, and that includes a rich man getting into heaven. Yet even Jesus said in John 5, I can of my own self do nothing. He only does what he sees and hears the Father say and do. So, we must humble ourselves (maybe even with fasting) and realize the truth that we are nothing without God.

Revelation 3:17 (KJV) says, "Because thou sayest, I am rich, and increased with goods, and have need of nothing; and knowest not that thou art wretched, and miserable, and poor, and blind, and naked." With humility comes more grace. With humility comes wisdom. With humility comes the strength to endure. For with God, nothing shall be impossible! It didn't work when I was haughty, not gentle, and weighed down in sin and disobedience. Once I humbly submitted myself to God and His will, things started manifesting for me. Friends, family, and church family even started to say how much faith I had and ask me questions about it. I was taken aback at first because I still vividly recalled nothing really working for me, so then I would say it's not me, it's God's grace. I'm not sure if they believed me, but I had learned that it truly is God making things work. All I had to do was hear, believe, and obey.

Joy in obedience

Speaking of obedience, there's almost a heaviness and weight when we think about being obedient and submission, but every good gift and perfect gift is from our Father. There is joy in obedience! So, whatever He tells us to do is the best thing for us. Whenever I think about doing the will of God, the enemy comes to try and make things hard for me to keep me from doing it. For example, 1 Thessalonians 5:18 (KJV) says, "In everything give thanks: for this is the will of God in Christ Jesus concerning you." Colossians 3:17 (KJV) says, "And whatsoever ye do in word or deed, do all in the name of the Lord Jesus, giving thanks to God and the Father by him."

I saw the phrase "thanksliving" somewhere, and it stuck with me. Live a life that is filled with thankfulness. Even if it's a horrible situation, we can still be thankful that Holy Spirit is with us and will never leave us while we're going through it because giving thanks is the will of God. So, if I'm working at a job I don't like, give thanks. If I'm on the way to church or work, and my car breaks down, give thanks. If my spouse cheats on me, give thanks. If I lose my job, give thanks. If I get that MRI and they find something wrong in my brain, give thanks. If the doctor gives my loved one a bad report, give thanks. If my child is sick or injured, give thanks. It is HARD! Yet, in those moments of trial and tribulation, we push through the situation and stand on the Word that we get the victory. Psalms 30:2-5 (KJV) says, "O Lord my God, I cried unto thee, and thou hast healed me. O Lord, thou hast brought up my soul from the grave: thou hast kept me alive, that I should not go down to the pit. Sing unto the Lord, O ye saints of his, and give thanks at the remembrance of his holiness. For his anger endureth but a moment, in his favor is life: weeping may endure for a night, but joy cometh in the morning." By giving thanks, we are believing by faith that joy will come, and we reckon that the sufferings of this present time are not worthy of being compared with the glory which shall be revealed in us!

05

CHAPTER

My Temptations

This entire time, I've been talking about God saying this and hearing God about that and asking God this other thing because being able to hear from God is essential to the life of a Christian. It is literally a matter of life and death for us. Just because a scripture comes to mind doesn't mean it's God. It could be the enemy trying to misuse scripture to justify doing something like he did with Jesus in the garden of Gethsemane. My pastor teaches that a basic and simple way to start down the path of hearing God is to put what you're hearing into three categories: God, Satan, and Self. If we can at least put our thoughts or images into those three sections, we are well on our way to clearly hearing God and not walking around in the dark.

When it's God speaking, it will line up with the Word and have characteristics found in James 3:17 (NKJV). It will be pure, peaceable, gentle, willing to yield, full of mercy and good fruits, without partiality and hypocrisy.

When it's Satan speaking, it will have characteristics found in James 3:14-16 (KJV) and John 10:10 (KJV), bitterness, strife, envy, jealousy, lying, stealing, killing, and destroying.

When it's Self, there are the self-focused thoughts such as "I'm hungry, what do I want to eat" or "What should I wear today" but overall, it will sound like whatever you've been feeding it. Matthew 12 says from the abundance of the heart, the mouth speaks. So if you've been reading and hearing the Word, praying, or fasting, then it will sound more like God and have characteristics like Him, but if you haven't, it will sound like Satan and his characteristics.

God never said that

Earlier, I brought up the Israelites as an example of a rebellious heart; let's keep going in that text. Numbers 14:40 (NLT) says, "Then they got up early the next morning and went to the top of the range of hills. "Let's go," they said. "We realize that we have sinned, but now we are ready to enter the land the Lord has promised us." Now it sounds like they're finally doing the right thing, and this could be any of us. We heard the Word but didn't do it, and now we're ready to do what God has said so He can fulfill His promises. But if they've admitted their sin and are doing what God said, why didn't it work? Because He has now said that they need to turn back and go into the wilderness. THAT is what will work. We cannot have faith in something God isn't telling us to do, and we need to watch that we don't miss what God IS saying by focusing on what He HAD said. God is so merciful that He even told them again not to go because He wasn't with them.

In Numbers 14:41-45 (KJV), Moses said, "Wherefore now do ye transgress the commandment of the Lord? But it shall not prosper. Go not up, for the Lord is not among you; that ye be not smitten before your enemies. For the Amalekites and the Canaanites are there before you, and ye shall fall by the sword: because ye are turned away from the Lord, therefore the Lord will not be with you. But they presumed to go up unto the hilltop…then the Amalekites came down, and the Canaanites which dwelt in that hill, and smote them, and discomfited them, even unto Hormah."

Again, we cannot have faith in something God isn't telling us to do; it won't work. It will instead cause us harm, and we will look foolish, just like the sons of Sceva in Acts 19. If God told you to do something three years ago and you finally get around to doing it, you should check with God to make sure you did not miss the window of opportunity. Now you may need to do something else; otherwise, you'll be in rebellion, and it won't work. God tells us that what WILL work is His Word. Isaiah 55:11 (NLT) says "It is the same with my word. I send it out, and it always produces fruit. It will accomplish all I want it to, and it will prosper everywhere I send it."

BUT speak the Word only

"And when Jesus was entered into Capernaum, there came unto him a centurion, beseeching him, and saying, Lord, my servant lieth at home sick of the palsy, grievously tormented. And Jesus saith unto him, 'I will come and heal him.' The centurion answered and said, 'Lord, I am not worthy that thou shouldest come under my roof: but speak the word only, and my servant shall be healed...' When Jesus heard it, he marveled, and said to them that followed, 'Verily I say unto you, I have not found so great faith, no, not in Israel....' And Jesus said unto the centurion, 'Go thy way; and as thou hast believed, so be it done unto thee.' And his servant was healed in the selfsame hour" Matthew 8:5-13 (KJV).

Can you imagine Jesus marveling at how great your faith is? We need to know what God is saying to us and be anchored in that. Only then can things work for us every time without fail. Once we receive the Word, we stand on it and are unmovable in our belief that it will come to pass. The centurion knew that all he needed was for Jesus to speak the Word, and it would be done, and he wasn't even Jewish! Have you ever had someone who isn't even a Christian have more faith than you that something would happen?

Imagine your pastor is standing before a group of people and telling them about the kingdom of God. Then somebody comes in and you know they aren't Christian, so you're wondering why they are there. They interrupt and say, my friend is sick in the hospital, and your pastor says okay, let me go to the hospital with you, but then that person says, oh no, you don't have to come, just pray for him right where you are, and he'll be healed. Wow! When we have a friend or loved one sick in the hospital, how many times do we ask our pastor or elders to come and pray for them? Compared to how often do we say there's no need to come, just speak the Word, and they will be healed? Or how many times do we say we're standing on the Word, but we haven't received the anointed spoken utterance from the Lord regarding our specific situation yet. We just pick what we think is an applicable scripture and start standing, but we missed the step of God speaking the Word first! We have to hear from Him first, and THEN we can believe and stand.

Satan comes to steal, kill, and destroy

When I was focusing on this story, immediately the enemy said, but that's Jesus, He can do that. Or that was back then. Or that type of miraculous healing doesn't happen anymore. Satan comes in quickly and tries to steal your faith by placing thoughts of doubt in your mind every single time. Just like the parable of the sower: "When anyone heareth the Word of the kingdom, and understandeth it not, then cometh the wicked one, and catcheth away that which was sown in his heart. This is he which received seed by the wayside." Matthew 13:19 (KJV). But Jesus himself said that we will do more things than Him because He goes to see the

Father. So yes, we can do it, too, and yes, those things are still happening and can still happen because we're not the ones doing it. It's the WORD that's working, causing things to change in the natural and putting our ministering angels in action.

We are in a battle, and these flaming arrows of doubt are constantly being shot at us like in Psalms 91, and we need the shield of faith to be protected against it. Sometimes we can hear something, and feel the fire burning on the inside of us, and the more we hear it and think about it, the bigger the fire grows and the more excited we start to feel. Then here comes Satan with a bucket of cold doubt water and with the cares of this world ready to douse our flames and quench the Holy Spirit. Just like in the parable of the sower from Luke 8:13 (NLT) that says "The seeds on the rocky soil represent those who hear the message and receive it with joy. But since they don't have deep roots, they believe for a while, then they fall away when they face temptation". They fall away as soon as they have problems or are persecuted for believing God's Word.

Satan is like a roaring lion seeking whom he may devour and when we are a prime target when you get filled with the Word because then you are fattened up in the spirit realm and filled with faith. He's despicable. He's the enemy of our soul. He's a thief, and there's nothing but strife, stealing, killing, and destruction when he's around. We should treat him like the worst scum on earth. He must be immediately chased out when he comes around, and we have nothing to do with him.

The Word says Satan brings strife and pride among brethren and chief friends. Our guard needs to be up constantly. In my head, I see a big dog lying down in the house, then a noise happens outside, and I can see him suddenly sit up stiff and alert and focusing on what that noise was. Sometimes the dog will lay back down once he realizes there's no threat, but other times he gets up and starts barking. That's how I imagine being on watch and sensitive to what's happening. When I'm meditating and thinking about the Word and feeling the movement of the Holy Spirit, then suddenly there's fear or doubt, then like a watchdog, I need to sit up and pay attention so I can make sure the enemy does not enter. Or if I'm hanging out with friends and family, and the conversation turns, and we start gossiping, or strife begins to come in. Something in me needs to sit up and become alert, just like that dog. Psalms 16:28 (KJV) states, "A froward man soweth strife: and a whisperer separateth chief friends." James 4:1 (NLT) says, "What is causing the quarrels and fights among you? Don't they come from the evil desires at war within you?"

When temptation comes

I tend to have a more logical and numbers-oriented mind, so when I need to hear God quickly and drown out other voices, particularly my own, a quick way is for me to pick a song and start to praise and dance to it because it shuts down the analytical side of my brain and opens up my creative side. For others, it may be singing, taking a shower, drinking tea while listening to worship or soaking music. You have to search and find what works for you. To be clear, fasting is always a way to put my flesh under, but sometimes I need an answer quickly, and a quick praise and dance works for me. You need to find what works for you as a quick way to reset your mind and heart.

To continue with the parable of the sower, Matthew 13:22-23 (KJV) says, "He also that received seed among the thorns is he that heareth the word; and the care of this world, and the deceitfulness of riches, choke the word, and he becometh unfruitful. But he that received seed into the good ground is he that heareth the Word, and understandeth it, which also beareth fruit, and bringeth forth, some a hundredfold, some sixty, some thirty." This is the same Word the centurion talked about when he said, "...but speak the Word only." So, when Satan, persecution, or the cares of this world remove the Word from our hearts, it doesn't work. But the Word WILL cause a return of a hundred, sixty, or thirtyfold in our lives. We just need to know the Word for us that is causing the return and believe that one and don't let anything take it from us.

When it comes to the Word of God, we must be rooted and unshakeable in our belief that it is true. Regardless of what has happened in the past or what it looks like in the present, our answer needs to be BUT speak the Word only Lord, and from there, we believe that whatever He says will work for us. Here are five of the many things that we are tempted to do when God has spoken the Word, and we're supposed to be believing:

1. **Get out of God's timing**- We are tempted to get out of the will of God by putting Him on our time, and if things don't happen when we expect it to, then we take matters into our own hands, or our faith starts to waver in what God told us. But there is a season for everything. Sometimes we need to let patience have her perfect work in us to be perfect and entire, not lacking anything. Isaiah prophesied about Jesus 700 years before He was born. Abraham had Isaac 25 years after God said He would give him a son. Jesus cursed the fig tree, and the next day it was dried up from the roots. Paul told the crippled man to stand up, and he immediately began walking. We need to move in God's time.

2. **Quit**- We are tempted to quit pressing toward the mark, quit our assignments, or even quit the faith altogether. Let us not grow weary in well-doing, for we shall reap if we faint not! Jesus said in this world we shall have tribulation but be of good cheer because he has overcome the world.

3. **Murmur/complain**- We are tempted to complain during the process but remember that it is an honor to serve God. 1 Corinthians 10:10-11 (KJV) says, "Neither murmur ye, as some of them also murmured, and were destroyed of the destroyer. Now all these things happened unto them for ensamples: and they are written for our admonition, upon whom the ends of the world are come."

4. **Fear**- We are tempted to fear. Fear that it won't work or even fear what will happen if it actually works and our life completely changes. In 2 Timothy 1:7 (KJV) it states, "For God hath not given us the spirit of fear, but of power, and of love, and of a sound mind."

5. **Make assumptions**- We are tempted to assume that it's not working or that faith stuff doesn't work because we didn't see the result or because Bishop A, Pastor B, and Prophet C prayed for the situation, and nothing happened. Yet Matthew 17:16 (KJV) says, "And I brought him to thy disciples, and they could not cure him." If the

man stopped at the disciples, his son would have never gotten cured. Or we're like Naaman in 2 Kings 5 (KJV) which says, "So Naaman came with his horses and with his chariot and stood at the door of the house of Elisha. And Elisha sent a messenger unto him, saying, Go and wash in Jordan seven times, and thy flesh shall come again to thee, and thou shalt be clean. But Naaman was wroth, and went away, and said, 'Behold, I thought, He will surely come out to me, and stand, and call on the name of the Lord his God, and strike his hand over the place, and recover the leper. Are not Abana and Pharpar, rivers of Damascus, better than all the waters of Israel? May I not wash in them and be clean?' So, he turned and went away in a rage." We assume that God will do it a certain way, so we miss what He actually did or is trying to do. We make assumptions and we miss the supernatural or spiritual, looking for the spectacular or dramatic.

When the winds blow

Just like when Jesus was walking on water as written in Matthew 14:28-31 (BSB), "'Lord, if it is You,' Peter replied, 'Command me to come to You on the water.' 'Come,' said Jesus. Then Peter got out of the boat, walked on the water, and came toward Jesus. But when he saw the strength of the wind, he was afraid, and beginning to sink, cried out, 'Lord, save me!' Immediately Jesus reached out His hand and took hold of Peter. 'You of little faith,' He said, 'Why did you doubt?'" Sometimes, we think more highly of ourselves than we ought to, as if we're above the disciples, and we wouldn't make the same mistakes they would. We think that if Jesus himself told us to walk on water, we would be filled with faith and not have any problems, but if things aren't working for us and we know that we heard from God, maybe we're just like Peter. We ask (command me to come to You on the water), and the Word gives instruction (come), and we start fine, then the winds get strong, and we change our focus and start sinking. Whatever the strong wind looks like for you–your child or family asking for money or getting into some sort of trouble, a good-looking person trying to get you to fornicate, a sale on shoes or clothes, a new car, a new technological device, unhealthy food, wanting more sleep, being anxious over when it's going to happen–these things make us take our focus off Jesus, off the Word that was spoken, and off the mark we're supposed to be pressing toward. Then we start sinking and calling for help and maybe even blaming God.

06

CHAPTER

We Are Victorious

On this journey of growing from faith to faith, the Lord helped me to see that He is for me and that He always causes me to triumph! We live in a dying, fallen world filled with sin and disobedience, so maybe the Lord did tell your manager to promote you, but they were disobedient. Maybe the Lord did tell that person to marry you, but they ignored Him and were disobedient. Maybe the Lord told your loved ones to exercise more, eat better, and go to the doctor so they can get healthy, but they were disobedient. Maybe the Lord set that property or that contract or that job aside for you, but the person over it was racist or sexist or just plain mean, so they ignored Him and were disobedient.

When something is not working, the issue is never God; He's perfect. Not only is He perfect, but He loves us with an everlasting love and will keep working and sending His ministering spirits to work on our behalf to cause things to happen for us. Isaiah 49:15 (NIV) says, "Can a mother forget the baby at her breast and have no compassion on the child she has borne? Though she may forget, I will not forget you!" Even if we have messed up in the past, we can have hope for better results next time because all things work together for the good of those who love God and have been called according to His purpose. So, I pray that this book was a help to you, and I will end it with a prayer that you can pray over yourself as we continue this journey together:

God, you are MY Heavenly Father, You are Jehovah, You are all-knowing and all-powerful, You are the I am that I am, the King of kings, the Alpha and Omega, the author and finisher of our faith, You are the ancient of days, You are God, and there is no other; You are God, and there is none like You. Declaring the end from the beginning and from ancient times things that are not yet done. God, I worship You! My soul shall boast in the Lord: the humble shall hear thereof and be glad.

Lord, I put on the whole armor of God that I may be able to stand and, having done all to stand. I gird my waist with truth. I put on the breastplate of righteousness, my feet are fitted with the preparation of the gospel of peace, I arm myself with the shield of faith, the helmet of salvation, and the sword of the Spirit. God, I repent for my unbelief in You, my deceitful heart, my disobedience, and my sins. I believe, receive, and thank You for forgiveness, righteousness, sanctification, and cleansing with the washing of water by the word. I thank you for showing me where I was missing it, so now I can walk in love by faith and complete my assignment. Thank You for showing me personally, specifically, and in detail, the areas I need to correct so that I can see You move in my life. Thank You for purifying my motives and giving me a new heart that's fertile ground for Your Word to take root. I believe by faith that though I have not seen it, it will come to pass.

I will revenge my disobedience when my obedience is fulfilled! I believe that You are working things out for my good, and even when the enemy is trying to keep the word from manifesting in my life, Your word says in Matthew 16:19 (ESV), "I will give you the keys of the kingdom of heaven, and whatever you bind on earth shall be bound in heaven, and whatever you loose on earth shall be loosed in heaven."

So, I bind up a hardened, unwilling, and unclean heart and loose a heart of flesh. I bind up unbelief, imposter syndrome, and I loose wisdom from above and real sincere faith that pleases God. I bind disobedience, pride, unforgiveness, envy, jealousy, rebellion, and I loose submission, humility, gentleness, joy, peace, and temperance. I bind the temptation to quit, complain, fear, and operate in my timing, and I loose God's timing, perseverance, and love. I bind up the hand of the enemy working against me, and I loose God's ministering spirits to go and minister for me—an heir of salvation—and cause finances or whatever I need to come, in the name of Jesus!

Your name is a strong tower. The righteous run into it and are safe, so I call on the name of Jesus, and I thank You for the gentle, warm, all-encompassing protection, safety, and love. You love me so much, You know the number of hairs on my head. You love me so much that if I should count the number of precious thoughts

You have of me, they are more in number than the grains of sand. You love me so much that You rejoice over me with singing. You love me so much that I should be called a child of God.

You love me so much that neither death nor life, neither angels nor demons, neither the present nor the future, nor any powers, neither height nor depth, nor anything else in all creation, will be able to separate me from Your love that is in Christ Jesus. Father, You love me so much, that while I was yet a sinner, You sent your only begotten Son, Jesus, to die for my sins, and because I believe in Jesus, I shall not perish but have everlasting life in eternity with You. Thank You for Your love! I cover this prayer, myself, my purpose, and all those whose destiny is attached to mine in the blood of Jesus. In Jesus' name, Amen!

About the Author

Tiffany McCormick is a loving wife, wonderful mother, fabulous daughter, and the best big sister ever. She's a born and raised Georgia Peach, where she attended primary and secondary school in Dekalb County and then graduated from the Georgia Institute of Technology with a B.S. in Applied Mathematics and a minor in Economics. She's currently pursuing her dual master's degree in Business Administration and Public Administration at Kennesaw State University, where she wants to aid in the creation of public-private partnerships that benefit the exploited and underprivileged.

In addition, Tiffany is a real estate investor and the current owner of Grand Slam Pizza Kennesaw. She is an active vessel in her church, the Hand of the Lord International in Decatur, GA, where she is an usher and a member of the Dollars and Sense team that hosts programs to help teach the community financial literacy. She gets excited when she's able to use the gifts God has given her to teach and talk about the economy and finances in a simple and easy-to-understand way that helps people learn what do to and start having conversations about wealth generation and investing God's way.